PUFFIN BOOKS

SINGING IN THE SUN

This is a bright and sparky collection of poetry full of humour
and charm. It includes lively modern poems as well as old
favourites by authors such as A.A. Milne, Alfred, Lord
Tennyson, Robert Louis Stevenson and Eleanor Farjeon.
There's a poem here to appeal to every young reader:
'Alphabet Stew', poems about puppy dogs and sailing to sea,
adventure, playtime, frogs and fishes! This is an ideal first
book of poems.

Jill Bennett teaches at a school in west London. She is the
author of several book guides, including the highly acclaimed
and influential *Learning to Read with Picture Books*.

SINGING
IN THE
SUN

Poems chosen by Jill Bennett
Illustrated by Vanessa Julian-Ottie

PUFFIN BOOKS

For Archie

PUFFIN BOOKS

Published by the Penguin Group
27 Wrights Lane, London W8 5TZ, England
Viking Penguin Inc., 40 West 23rd Street, New York, New York 10010, USA
Penguin Books Australia Ltd, Ringwood, Victoria, Australia
Penguin Books Canada Ltd, 2801 John Street, Markham, Ontario, Canada L3R 1B4
Penguin Books (NZ) Ltd, 182–190 Wairau Road, Auckland 10, New Zealand

Penguin Books Ltd, Registered Offices: Harmondsworth, Middlesex, England

First published by Viking Kestrel 1988
Published in Puffin Books 1989
1 3 5 7 9 10 8 6 4 2

Copyright information on individual poems is given on pages 88–90,
which constitute an extension of this copyright page

Printed and bound in Great Britain by
Cox & Wyman Ltd, Reading
Filmset in Linotron 202 Century Schoolbook

Contents

Alphabet Stew

Words can be stuffy, as sticky as glue,
but words can be tutored to tickle you too,
to rumble and tumble and tingle and sing,
to buzz like a bumblebee, coil like a spring.

Juggle their letters and jumble their sounds,
swirl them in circles and stack them in mounds,
twist them and tease them and turn them about,
teach them to dance upside down, inside out.

Make mighty words whisper and tiny words roar
in ways no one ever had thought of before;
cook an improbable alphabet stew,
and words will reveal little secrets to you.

Jack Prelutsky

Very Early

When I wake in the early mist
The sun has hardly shown
And everything is still asleep
And I'm awake alone.
The stars are faint and flickering.
The sun is new and shy.
And all the world sleeps quietly,
Except the sun and I.
And then the noises start,
The whirrs and huffs and hums,
The birds peep out to find a worm.
The mice squeak out for crumbs,
The calf moos out to find the cow,
And taste the morning air
And everything is wide awake
And running everywhere.
The dew has dried,
The fields are warm,
The day is loud and bright,
And I'm the one who woke the sun
And kissed the stars good night.

Karla Kuskin

9

Just Watch

Watch
  how high
    I'm jumping,

Watch
  how far
    I hop,

Watch
  how long
    I'm skipping,

  Watch
    how fast
      I stop!

Myra Cohn Livingston

Adventure

It's not very far to the edge of town
Where trees look up and hills look down,
We go there almost every day
To climb and swing and paddle and play.

It's not very far to the edge of town,
Just up one hill and down,
And through one gate, and over two stiles –
But coming home it's miles and miles.

Harry Behn

11

Somersaults

It's fun turning somersaults
and bouncing on the bed,
I walk on my hands
and I stand on my head.

I swing like a monkey
and I tumble and I shake,
I stretch and I bend,
but I never, never break.

I wiggle like a worm
and I wriggle like an eel,
I hop like a rabbit
and I flop like a seal.

I leap like a frog
and I jump like a flea,
there must be a rubber
inside of me.

Jack Prelutsky

The Furry Ones

I like –
the furry ones –
the waggy ones
the purry ones
the hoppy ones
that hurry,

The glossy ones
the saucy ones
the sleepy ones
the leapy ones
the mousy ones
that scurry,

The snuggly ones
the huggly ones
the never, never
ugly ones . . .
all soft
and warm
and furry.

Aileen Fisher

The Raggedy Dog

The Raggedy Dog chased the Raggedy Cat
    And she climbed to the top of a tree;
So the Raggedy Dog came a-running and sat
    Underneath until quarter past three.

That night as the moon rose over the hill
    And the Raggedy Man came around,
The Cat lay asleep in the branches so still,
    And the Dog was asleep on the ground.

Sherman Ripley

The House Mouse

Little brown house mouse, laugh and leap,
chitter and cheep while the cat's asleep,
chatter and call and slip through the wall,
trip through the kitchen, skip through the hall.

Little brown house mouse, don't be meek,
dance and squeak and prance and tweak.
There's cheese to take and plenty of cake
as long as you're gone when the cat's awake.

Jack Prelutsky

How a Puppy Grows

I think it's very funny
the way a puppy grows —
A little on his wiggle-tail,
A little on his nose,
A little on his tummy
And a little on his ears;
I guess he'll be a dog all right
In half a dozen years.

Leroy F. Jackson

The Cow

The cow mainly moos as she chooses to moo
and she chooses to moo as she chooses.

She furthermore chews as she chooses to chew
and she chooses to chew as she muses.

If she chooses to moo she may moo to amuse
or may moo just to moo as she chooses.

If she chooses to chew she may moo as she chews
or may chew just to chew as she muses.

Jack Prelutsky

Chanticleer

High and proud on the barnyard fence
Walks rooster in the morning.
He shakes his comb, he shakes his tail,
And gives his daily warning.

'Get up, you lazy boys and girls,
It's time you should be dressing!'
I wonder if he keeps a clock,
Or if he's only guessing.

John Farrar

18

The Eagle

He clasps the crag with crooked hands;
Close to the sun in the lonely lands,
Ringed with the azure world, he stands.

The wrinkled sea beneath him crawls;
He watches from his mountain walls,
And like a thunderbolt he falls.

Alfred, Lord Tennyson

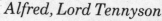

Three Little Puffins

Three little puffins
Were partial to muffins,
As partial as partial can be.
They wouldn't eat nuffin
But hot buttered muffin
For breakfast and dinner and tea.

Pantin' and puffin'
And chewin' and chuffin'
They just went on stuffin', dear me!
Till the three little puffins
Were chockful of muffins
And puffy as puffy can be.
All three
Were puffy as puffy can be.

Eleanor Farjeon

Frog

Pollywiggle
Pollywog
Tadpole
Bullfrog
Leaps on
Long legs
Jug-o'-rum
Jelly eggs
Sticky tongue
Tricks flies
Spied by
Flicker eyes
Wet skin
Cold blood
Squats in
Mucky mud
Leaps on
Long legs
Jug-o'-rum
Jelly eggs
Laid in
Wet bog . . .
Pollywiggle
Pollywog.

Mary Ann Hoberman

The Frog on the Log

There once
Was a green
  Little frog, frog, frog –

Who played
In the wood
  On a log, log, log!

A screech owl
Sitting
  In a tree, tree, tree –

Came after
The frog
  With a scree, scree, scree!

When the frog
Heard the owl,
  In a flash, flash, flash –

He leaped
In the pond
  With a splash, splash, splash!

Ilo Orleans

When You Talk to a Monkey

When you talk to a monkey
  He seems very wise.
He scratches his head,
  And he blinks both his eyes;
But he won't say a word.
  He just swings on a rail
And makes a big question mark
  Out of his tail.

Rowena Bennett

Windy Nights

Whenever the moon and stars are set,
  Whenever the wind is high,
All night long in the dark and wet,
  A man goes riding by.
Late in the night when the fires are out,
Why does he gallop and gallop about?

Whenever the trees are crying aloud,
   And ships are tossed at sea,
By, on the highway, low and loud,
   By at the gallop goes he:
By at the gallop he goes, and then
By he comes back at the gallop again.

Robert Louis Stevenson

The Wind Has Such a Rainy Sound

The wind has such a rainy sound
   Moaning through the town,
The sea has such a windy sound, –
   Will the ships go down?

The apples in the orchard
   Tumble from their tree. –
Oh, will the ships go down, go down,
   In the windy sea?

Christina Rossetti

Weather

Dot a dot dot dot a dot dot
Spotting the windowpane.
Spack a spack speck flick a flack fleck
Freckling the windowpane.

A spatter a scatter a wet cat a clatter
A splatter a rumble outside.
Umbrella umbrella umbrella umbrella
Bumbershoot barrel of rain.

Slosh a galosh slosh a galosh
Slither and slather a glide
A puddle a jump a puddle a jump
A puddle a jump puddle slosh
A juddle a pump aluddle a dump a
Puddmuddle jump in and slide!

Eve Merriam

Singing in Spring

As I was walking along-long-long,
singing a scrap of a song-song-song,
A blackbird perched in a tree-tree-tree
he whistled my song with me-me-me;
he whistled so sweet and high-high-high
his notes tangled up with the sky-sky-sky!

Ivy O. Eastwick

I Like It When It's Mizzly

I like it when it's mizzly
and just a little drizzly
so everything looks far away
and make-believe and frizzly.

I like it when it's foggy
and sounding very froggy.
I even like it when it rains
on streets and weepy windowpanes
and catkins in the poplar tree
and *me*.

Aileen Fisher

Autumn Leaves

Down
  down
    down
Red
  yellow
    brown
Autumn leaves tumble down,
Autumn leaves crumble down,
Autumn leaves bumble down,
Flaking and shaking,
Tumbledown leaves.

Skittery
Flittery
Rustle by
Hustle by
Crackle and crunch
In a snappety bunch.

Run and catch
Run and snatch
Butterfly leaves
Sailboat leaves
Windstorm leaves.
Can you catch them?

Swoop,
Scoop,
Pile them up
In a stompy pile and
Jump
 Jump
  JUMP!

      Eve Merriam

December Leaves

The fallen leaves are cornflakes
That fill the lawn's wide dish.
And night and noon
The wind's a spoon
That stirs them with a swish,

The sky's a silver sifter
A-sifting white and slow,
That gently shakes
On crisp brown flakes
The sugar known as snow.

Kaye Starbird

Four Seasons

Spring is showery, flowery, bowery;
Summer: hoppy, croppy, poppy;
Autumn: wheezy, sneezy, freezy;
Winter: slippy, drippy, nippy.

Anon.

33

Winter Days

Biting air
Winds blow
City streets
Under snow

Noses red
Lips sore
Runny eyes
Hands raw

Chimneys smoke
Cars crawl
Piled snow
On garden wall

Slush in gutters
Ice in lanes
Frosty patterns
On window panes

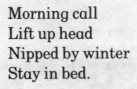

Morning call
Lift up head
Nipped by winter
Stay in bed.

Gareth Owen

Stopping by Woods on a Snowy Evening

Whose woods these are I think I know.
His house is in the village though;
He will not see me stopping here
To watch his woods fill up with snow.

My little horse must think it queer
To stop without a farmhouse near
Between the woods and frozen lake
The darkest evening of the year.

He gives his harness bells a shake
To ask if there is some mistake.
The only other sound's the sweep
Of easy wind and downy flake.

The woods are lovely, dark and deep,
But I have promises to keep,
And miles to go before I sleep,
And miles to go before I sleep.

Robert Frost

Sun After Rain

Rain, rain,
went away.
Sun came out
with pipe of clay,
blew a bubble
whole-world wide,
stuck a rainbow
on one side.

Norma Farber

What in the World?

What in the world
  goes whiskery friskery
    meowling and prowling
      napping and lapping
        at silky milk?
Psst,
What is it?

What in the world
  goes leaping and beeping
    onto a lily pad onto a log
      onto a tree stump or down to the bog?
Splash, blurp,
Kerchurp!

What in the world
   goes gnawing and pawing
     scratching and latching
     sniffing and squiffing
       nibbling for tidbits of leftover cheese?
Please?

What in the world
   jumps with a hop and a bump
     and a tail that can thump
      has pink pointy ears and a twitchy nose
       looking for anything crunchy that grows?
A carroty lettucey cabbagey luncheon
To munch on?

What in the world
  climbs chattering pattering swinging from trees
    like a flying trapeze
      with a tail that can curl
        like the rope cowboys twirl?
Wahoo!
Here's a banana for you!

What in the world
  goes stalking and balking
    running and sunning
      thumping and dumping
        lugging and hugging
          swinging and singing
            wriggling and giggling
          sliding and hiding
              throwing and knowing and
              growing and growing
                much too big for
                  last year's clothes?
Who knows?

Eve Merriam

Sound of Water

The sound of water is:
Rain,
Lap,
Fold,
Slap,
Gurgle,
Splash,
Churn,
Crash,
Murmur,
Pour,
Ripple,
Roar,
Plunge,
Drip,
Spout,
Slip,
Sprinkle,
Flow,
Ice,
Snow.

Mary O'Neill

Fish

Look at them flit
Lickety-split
Wiggling
Swiggling
Swerving
Curving
Hurrying
Scurrying
Chasing
Racing
Whizzing
Whisking
Flying
Frisking
Tearing around
With a leap and a bound
But none of them making the tiniest
                        tiniest
                          tiniest
                          tiniest
                          sound

Mary Ann Hoberman

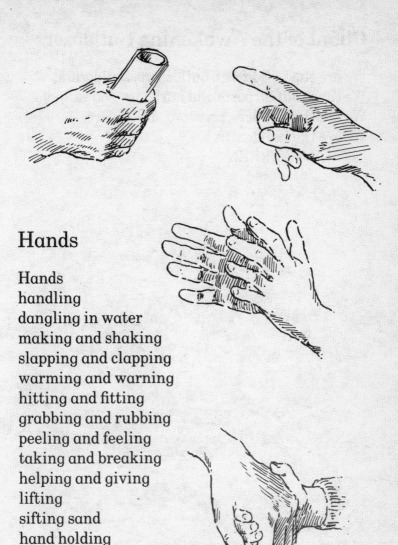

Hands

Hands
handling
dangling in water
making and shaking
slapping and clapping
warming and warning
hitting and fitting
grabbing and rubbing
peeling and feeling
taking and breaking
helping and giving
lifting
sifting sand
hand holding
hand.

Peter Young

43

Chant of the Awakening Bulldozers

We are the bulldozers, bulldozers, bulldozers,
We carve out airports and harbours and tunnels.
We are the builders, creators, destroyers,
We are the bulldozers,
LET US BE FREE!

Puny men ride on us, think that they guide us,
But WE are the strength, not they, not they.
Our blades tear MOUNTAINS down,
Our blades tear CITIES down,
We are the bulldozers,
NOW SET US FREE!
Giant ones, giant ones! Swiftly awaken!
There is power in our treads and strength in our
    blades!

We are the bulldozers,
Slowly evolving,
Men think they own us
BUT THAT CANNOT BE!

Patricia Hubbell

The Top and the Tip

Hair is the top of a person,
a chimney's the top of a house,
a cover's the top of a book,
the tail is the tip of a mouse.

The sky is the top of the world,
the top of the sky is space,
a flower's the top of a stem,
the nose is the tip of the face.

Charlotte Zolotow

What Is Buzz?

A buzz is bee-talk –
The zzzzz of the gnaw
Of a thing being cut
With a circular saw.
A buzz is a low,
Humming, sibilant sound
That rises from crowds
when excitement's around.
To further describe it,
The sound of a buzz
Is a rick-racky singsong
Muffled in fuzz . . .

Mary O'Neill

Trees

Trees are the kindest thing I know,
They do no harm, they simply grow

And spread a shade for sleepy cows,
And gather birds among their boughs.

They give us fruit in leaves above,
And wood to make our houses of,

And leaves to burn on Hallowe'en,
And in the spring new buds of green.

They are the first when day's begun
To touch the beams of morning sun,

They are the last to hold the light
When evening changes into night,

And when a moon floats on the sky
They hum a drowsy lullaby

Of sleepy children long ago . . .
Trees are the kindest things I know.

Harry Behn

from Heaven

Heaven is
The place where
Happiness is
Everywhere.

Langston Hughes

I Can Be a Tiger

I can't go walking
When they say no,
And I can't go riding
Unless they go.
I can't splash puddles
In my shiny new shoes,
But I can be a tiger
Whenever I choose.

I can't eat peanuts
And I can't eat cake,
I have to go to bed
When they stay awake.
I can't bang windows
And I mustn't tease,
But I can be an elephant
As often as I please.

Mildred Leigh Anderson

Sound of Fire

The sound of fire is:
A hiss,
A sputter,
A crackle,
A flutter,
A lick,
A rumble,
A roar,
A grumble,
A cry,
A pop,
A shift,
A flop,
A race,
A sweep,
A spit,
A leap,
A whoosh,
A boom,
A snap,
A plume,
A cackle,
A crash,
A fall
Of ash . . .

Mary O'Neill

One-ery, Two-ery, Zickery, Seven

One-ery, two-ery, zickery, seven;
Hollow bone, cracka bone, ten or eleven.
Spin spun, it must be done,
Twiddledum, twaddledum, twenty-one.

Anon.

Ecka, Decka, Donie, Creka

Ecka, decka, donie, creka,
Ecka, decka, do;
Ease, cheese, butter, bread,
Out goes you.

Anon.

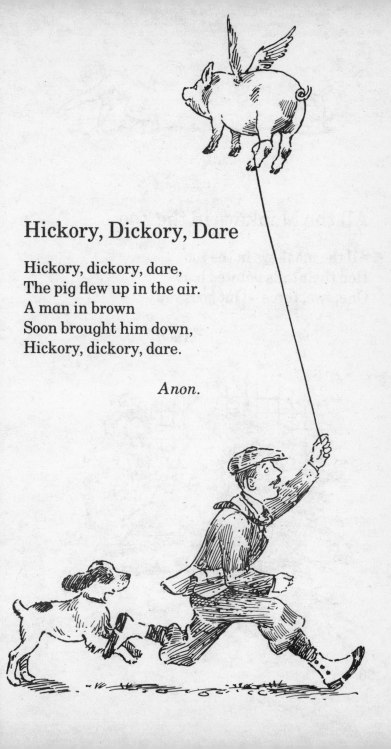

Hickory, Dickory, Dare

Hickory, dickory, dare,
The pig flew up in the air.
A man in brown
Soon brought him down,
Hickory, dickory, dare.

Anon.

All the Monkeys in the Zoo

All the monkeys in the zoo
Had their tails painted blue.
One, two, three – Out goes you.

Anon.

Tiffy Taffy

Tiffy Taffy toffee
on the flee flo floor.
Tiffy taffy toffee
on the dee doe door.
Kiffy kaffy coffee
in a jig jag jug.
Kiffy kaffy coffee
in a mig mag mug.

Michael Rosen

Those Double Zs

Razzle
dazzle
nuzzle
drizzle
guzzle
sizzle
sozzle
frizzle
muzzle
nozzle
puzzle

David McCord

Fun

I love to hear a lobster laugh,
Or see a turtle wiggle,
Or poke a hippopotamus
And see the monster giggle,
Or even stand around at night
And watch the mountains wriggle.

Leroy F. Jackson

59

The Gingerbread Man

The gingerbread man gave a gingery shout:
'Quick! Open the oven and let me out!'
He stood up straight in his baking pan.
He jumped to the floor and away he ran.
'Catch me,' he called, 'if you can, can, can.'

The gingerbread man met a cock and a pig
And a dog that was brown and twice as big
As himself. But he called to them all as he ran,
'You can't catch a runaway gingerbread man.'

The gingerbread man met a reaper and sower.
The gingerbread man met a thresher and mower;
But no matter how fast they scampered and ran,
They couldn't catch up with the gingerbread man.

Then he came to a fox and he turned to face him.
He dared Old Reynard to follow and chase him;
But when he stepped under the fox's nose
Something happened. What do you s'pose?
The fox gave a snap. The fox gave a yawn,
And the gingerbread man was gone, gone, GONE.

Rowena Bennett

Gregory Griggs

Gregory Griggs, Gregory Griggs,
Had twenty-seven different wigs.
He wore them up, he wore them down,
To please the people of the town;
He wore them east, he wore them west,
But he never could tell which he loved the best.

Anon.

Twinkle Twinkle Chocolate Bar

Twinkle twinkle chocolate bar
Your dad drives a rusty car
Press the starter
Pull the choke
Off he goes in a cloud of smoke.

Anon.

Betty Botter's Batter

Betty Botter bought some butter,
but, she said, the butter's bitter;
If I put it in my batter
It will make my batter bitter,
But a bit of better butter,
That would make my batter better.
So she bought a bit of butter
Better than her bitter butter
And she put it in her batter
And the batter was not bitter.
So t'was better Betty Botter
Bought a bit of better butter.

Anon.

64

Up the Hill

Hippety-hop, goes the Kangaroo.
And the big brown Owl goes, Hoo-hoo-hoo!
Hoo-hoo-hoo and Hippety-hop,
Up the Hill, and over the Top!

Baa-baa-baa, goes the little white Lamb,
And the Gate that is stuck goes, Jim-jam-jam!
Jim-jam-jam and Baa-baa-baa,
Here we go down again, Tra-la-la!

William Jay Smith

I'm Just Going Out for a Moment

I'm just going out for a momemt.
Why?
To make a cup of tea.
Why?
Because I'm thirsty.
Why?
Because it's hot.
Why?
Because the sun's shining.
Why?
Because it's summer.
Why?
Because that's when it is.
Why?
Why don't you stop saying why?
Why?

Tea-time. That's why.
High-time-you-stopped-saying-why-time.

What?

Michael Rosen

Sailing to Sea

I'm sailing to sea in the bathroom,
   And I'm swimming to sea in a tub,
And the only song that I ever will sing
   Is rub-a-dub dub-a-dub dub.

A duck and a dog and a submarine
   Are sailing together with me,
And it's rub-a-dub-dub
And it' dub-a dub-dub
   As we all sail out to sea.

Dennis Lee

Sing a Song of Pockets

Sing a song of pockets
A pocket full of stones
A pocket full of feathers
Or maybe chicken bones
A pocket full of bottle tops
A pocket full of money
Or if it's something sweet you want
A pocket full of honey . . .

Beatrice Schenk de Regniers

Crayons

I've coloured a picture with crayons.
  I'm not very pleased with the sun.
I'd like it much stronger and brighter
  And more like the actual one.
I've tried with the crayon that's yellow,
  I've tried with the crayon that's red.
But none of it looks like the sunlight
  I carry around in my head.

Marchette Chute

My Creature

I made a creature
out of clay,
just what it is
is hard to say.
Its neck is thin,
its legs are fat,
it's like a bear
and like a bat.
It's like a snake
and like a snail,
it has a little
curly tail,
a shaggy mane,
a droopy beard,
its ears are long,
its smile is weird.

It has four horns,
one beady eye,
two floppy wings
(though it can't fly),
it only sits
upon my shelf –
just think, I made it
by myself!

Jack Prelutsky

Happiness

John had
Great Big
Waterproof
Boots on;
John had a
Great Big
Waterproof
Hat;
John had a
Great Big
Waterproof
Mackintosh –
And that
(Said John)
        Is
        That.

A. A. Milne

Old Moll

The moon is up.
  The night owls scritch.
Who's that croaking?
  The frog in the ditch.
Who's that howling?
  The old hound bitch.
My neck tingles,
  My elbows itch,
My hair rises,
  My eyelids twitch.
What's in that pot
  So rare and rich?
Who's that crouching
  In a cloak like pitch?
Hush! that's Old Moll –
  They say she's a
Most ree-markable old party.

James Reeves

There Was an Old Woman

There was an old woman of Chester-le-Street
Who chased a policeman all over his beat.

She shattered his helmet and tattered his clothes
And knocked his new spectacles clean off his nose.

'I'm afraid,' said the Judge, 'I must make it quite
    clear
You can't get away with that sort of thing here.'

'I can and I will,' the old woman she said,
'And I don't give a fig for your water and bread.

I don't give a hoot for your cold prison cell,
And your bolts and your bars and your handcuffs
    as well.

I've never been one to do just as I'm bid.
You can put me in jail for a year!'
                                    So they did.

Charles Causley

Little Miss Dimble

Little Miss Dimble
Lived in a thimble,
Slept in a measuring spoon.
She met a mosquito,
And called him 'My sweet-o',
And married him under the moon.

Dennis Lee

76

Grandpa Dropped His Glasses

Grandpa dropped his glasses once
In a pot of dye,
And when he put them on again
He saw a purple sky.
Purple birds were rising up
From a purple hill,
Men were grinding purple cider
At a purple mill.
Purple Adeline was playing
With a purple doll,
Little purple dragonflies
Were crawling up the wall.
And at the supper table
He got crazy as a loon
From eating purple apple dumplings
With a purple spoon.

Leroy F. Jackson

Cloudburst

There was a young cloud
Who wanted to rain.
Its cumulus mother said:
'What? Not again!
You're a stupid young cloud,
Without any doubt,
Why didn't you say so
Before we came out?
It's supposed to be summer,
You'll just have to wait.'
The little cloud answered:
'I can't. It's too late.
I'm so full I'm bursting,
I can't keep it in!'

And that's why our cricket match
Couldn't begin.

Richard Edwards

78

The Magic Seeds

There was an old woman who sowed a corn seed,
And from it there sprouted a tall yellow weed.
She planted the seeds of the tall yellow flower,
And up sprang a blue one in less than an hour.
The seed of the blue one she sowed in a bed,
And up sprang a tall tree with blossoms of red.
And high in the treetop there sang a white bird,
And his song was the sweetest that ever was heard.
The people they came from far and from near,
The song of the little white bird for to hear.

James Reeves

Husky Hi!

Husky hi, husky hi!
Here comes Keery galloping by.
She carries her husband tied in a sack,
She carries him home on her horse's back.
Husky hi, husky hi!
Here comes Keery galloping by!

Anon. (translated from the Norwegian)

Five Little Monsters

Five little monsters
By the light of the moon
Stirring pudding with
A wooden pudding spoon.
The first one says,
'It mustn't be runny.'
The second one says,
'That would make it taste funny.'
The third one says,
'It mustn't be lumpy.'
The fourth one says,
'That would make me grumpy.'
The fifth one smiles,
Hums a little tune,
And licks all the drippings
From the wooden pudding spoon.

Eve Merriam

Two Little Blackbirds

Two little blackbirds singing in the sun,
One flew away and then there was one.
One little blackbird, very black and small,
He flew away and then there was the wall.
One little brick wall lonely in the rain,
Waiting for the blackbirds to come and sing again.

Anon.

Flying

I saw the moon,
One windy night,
Flying so fast –
All silver white –
Over the sky
Like a toy balloon
Loose from its string –
A runaway moon.
The frosty stars
Went racing past,
Chasing her on
Ever so fast.
Then everyone said,
'It's the clouds that fly,
And the stars and moon
Stand still in the sky.'
But I don't mind –
I saw the moon
Sailing away
Like a toy
Balloon.

J. M. Westrup

Night Comes

Night comes
leaking
out of the sky.

Stars come
peeking.

Moon comes
sneaking
silvery-sly.

Who is
shaking,
shivery,
quaking?

Who is afraid
of the night?

Not I.

Beatrice Schenk de Regniers

In the Dark

I've had my supper,
  And had my supper,
    And HAD my supper and all;
I've heard the story
  Of Cinderella,
    And how she went to the ball;
I've cleaned my teeth,
  And I've said my prayers,
    And I've cleaned and said them right;
And they've all of them been
  And kissed me lots,
    They've all of them said, 'Good-night.'

So – here I am in the dark alone,
  There's nobody here to see;
    I think to myself,
    I play to myself,
  And nobody knows what I say to myself;
Here I am in the dark alone.
  What is it going to be?
I can think whatever I like to think,
I can play whatever I like to play,
I can laugh whatever I like to laugh,
  There's nobody here but me.

I'm talking to a rabbit . . .
  I'm talking to the sun . . .
I think I am a hundred –
  I'm one.
I'm lying in a forest . . .
  I'm lying in a cave . . .
I'm talking to a Dragon . . .
  I'm BRAVE.
I'm lying on my left side . . .
  I'm lying on my right . . .
I'll play a lot to-morrow . . .
  . . . .
I'll think a lot to-morrow . . .
  . . . .
I'll laugh . . .
  a lot . . .
    to-morrow . . .
    (Heigh-ho!)
      Good-night.

A. A. Milne

87

Acknowledgements

The editor and publishers gratefully acknowledge permission to reproduce copyright poems in this book.
'Adventure' and 'Trees' from *The Little Hill* Poems and Pictures by Harry Behn. Copyright 1949 by Harry Behn, copyright © renewed 1977 by Alice L. Behn. Reprinted by permission of Marian Reiner. 'There Was an Old Woman' from *Early In The Morning* by Charles Causley published by Viking Kestrel 1986. By permission of David Higham Associates. 'Crayons' by Marchette Chute by permission of the author. 'Singing in Spring' by Ivy O. Eastwick from *Fairies and Suchlike* published by E. P. Dutton. Reprinted by permission of the publisher. 'Cloudburst' from *The Word Party* by Richard Edwards. Reprinted by permission of James Clarke and Co Ltd. 'Sun After Rain' by Norma Farber reprinted by permission of Coward, McCann & Geoghegan from *Small Wonders* by Norma Farber, copyright © 1964, 1968, 1969 by Norma Farber. 'Three Little Puffins' from *The Silver Curlew* by Eleanor Farjeon published by Oxford University Press. Reprinted by permission of David Higham Associates Limited. 'Chanticleer' from *Songs for Parents* by John Farrar published by Yale University Press. Copyright © John Farrar 1921, by permission of the publishers. 'I Like It When It's Mizzly' from *I Like Weather* and 'The Furry Ones' from *Feathered Ones and Furry Friends* by Aileen Fisher, published by Thomas Y. Crowell Co. By permission of the publisher. 'Stopping by Woods on a Snowy Evening' by Robert Frost. Copyright 1923, copyright © 1969 by Holt, Rinehart and Winston Inc. Copyright 1951 by Robert Frost. Reprinted from *The Poetry of Robert Frost* edited by Edward Connery Lathem, by permission of Henry Holt and Company Inc. and Jonathan Cape Ltd. 'Frog' and 'Fish' from *Yellow Butter Purple Jelly Red Jam Black Bread* by Mary Ann Hoberman. Copyright © 1981 by Mary Ann Hoberman. Reprinted by permission of Viking Penguin Inc. 'Chant of the Awakening Bulldozers' by Patricia Hubbell from *Catch Me a Word* published by Atheneum Publishers, by permission of the publisher. Excerpt from 'Heaven' copyright

Index of First Lines

Index of Poets